Alzheimer's Disease

Help for Families in Crisis

Robert Smith

New
Growth
Press

www.newgrowthpress.com

New Growth Press, Greensboro, NC 27404
www.newgrowthpress.com
Copyright © 2014 by Robert Smith

All Scripture quotations, unless otherwise indicated, are taken
from *The Holy Bible, English Standard Version*® (ESV®), copyright
© 2000, 2001 by Crossway Bibles, a division of Good News
Publishers. Used by permission. All rights reserved.
     Scripture quotations marked NIV are taken from the *Holy
Bible,* New International Version®, NIV®. Copyright © 1973, 1978,
1984, 2011 by Biblica, Inc. Used by permission. All rights reserved
worldwide.
     Scripture quotations marked NKJV are taken from the New
King James Version®. Copyright © 1982 by Thomas Nelson, Inc.
Used by permission. All rights reserved.

Cover Design: Faceout Books, faceoutstudio.com
Typesetting: Lisa Parnell, lparnell.com

ISBN: 978-1-939946-79-9 (Print)
ISBN: 978-1-939946-80-5 (eBook)

Library of Congress Cataloging-in-Publication Data
Smith, Robert, 1929–
  Alzheimer's disease : help for families in crisis / Robert Smith.
     pages cm
  ISBN 978-1-939946-79-9 — ISBN 978-1-939946-80-5 (ebook)
1. Caregivers—Religious life. 2. Caring—Religious aspects—
Christianity. 3. Alzheimer's disease—Patients—Home care.
4. Alzheimer's disease—Religious aspects—Christianity. I. Title.
 BV4910.9.S65 2014
 248.8'6196831—dc23
                                                              2014026237
Printed in Canada

21 20 19 18 17 16 15 14   1 2 3 4 5

"Grandpa, you put your car keys in the refrigerator."

What might have been a humorous mistake was unsettling to Joe's thirty-year-old grandson and to others in the Evans family. It was among a list of symptoms they had seen displayed in the family patriarch. Grandpa had lost his glasses, and the family found them on top of his study bookcase. At times he didn't seem to recognize where he was. The elderly gentleman was a seventy-five-year-old retired math teacher who had been active all his life, and even in retirement continued to enjoy golfing. The family wondered if there was a problem bigger than simple forgetfulness or absentmindedness after he had a series of events including turning the wrong way on his trip home from the golf course, failing to mail the letters lying on the front seat of his car, and not remembering the name of a close friend. Also disconcerting was that their usually kind, godly grandparent seemed to be more easily irritated than usual.

The refrigerator incident motivated them to seek medical attention, so they took him to their family doctor for a thorough physical exam. The absence of any potential treatable causes for memory problems—such as low thyroid hormone, vitamin B12 deficiency, brain tumor, stroke, or blood clots in the brain—was helpful but disappointing news. It was helpful to know he did not have any of those conditions, but it was disappointing to learn there was no treatment to reverse the condition. Though there was no specific test to confirm the disease, the doctor believed Joe was experiencing the early stages of Alzheimer's disease (AD).

If you have a loved one who has been diagnosed with AD, the above scenario may be all too familiar to you, even if the details are different. You are facing a multitude of questions regarding treatment and short- and long-term care options, as well as how you'll be able to handle the changes coming your way. Be reassured that God's grace will help you with each new stage you encounter.

As a family member and/or someone planning to help care for someone with Alzheimer's disease, you are also facing significant and life-altering challenges. Through all of the changes and challenges, remember that both you and your loved one have a Savior who knows what it's like to suffer and who offers his strength and his resources. Turn to him for the comfort Paul describes in 2 Corinthians 1:3–4: "Praise be to the God and Father of our Lord Jesus Christ, the Father of compassion and the God of all comfort, who comforts us in all our troubles, so that we can comfort those in any trouble with the comfort we ourselves receive from God" (NIV). Trust the God of comfort and wisdom to guide you in providing care for your loved one. Even though you do not know the specific problems the disease will produce, depend on God's Word and wisdom to guide you as you walk this path with them.

The Early Stages

Early on you will face the difficulty that there is no known cure or treatment for Alzheimer's disease—nothing will reverse or slow down the progression of your loved one's condition. As you learn about the disease affecting your loved one, you will find out that the brain is going through progressive, irreversible damage at the cellular level, which will affect memory, thinking, and learning skills, and is responsible for the mild memory problems you've probably already noticed. You'll also find that "as Alzheimer's advances through the brain, it leads to increasingly severe symptoms, including disorientation, mood and behavior changes; deepening confusion about events, time, and place; unfounded suspicions about family, friends, and professional caregivers; more serious memory loss and behavior changes; and difficulty speaking, swallowing, and walking."[1] While it is painful to think about your loved one going through these things, understanding the effects of the disease will help you think through potential problems and recognize that declining memory and ability to think and reason clearly, along with impaired judgment, will require the wisdom and grace of God to navigate. It is important to understand that there will come a time when your loved one will be unable to accomplish even simple tasks required for daily living, and it is helpful to begin preparing for this.

Even as you begin to wrestle with the reality of how this disease progresses, it is important to note that there are things you can do to help keep your loved one from deteriorating too rapidly. In the early stages of Alzheimer's, the person should "stay as engaged and active as possible for as long as possible."[2] One way to help loved ones with Alzheimer's stay engaged is to schedule family members and friends to spend time with them doing the activities they enjoy. For example, if someone has enjoyed checkers and dominos, play those games together. Even if the person is not able to plan and think through plays as in former years, he or she can still enjoy the game. Try to choose games or activities that require less short-term memory. You can also encourage and even join your loved one in appropriate levels of exercise, which is helpful to both the body and mind. Encourage their friends to join in these activities to help keep them engaged, active, and socially connected. These kinds of activities allow everyone who cares for them to enjoy time together.

The Middle Stages

As the disease progresses, your loved one will begin to experience decreased functioning in several ways. Each one will have its own challenges—both for you and for them. Recognizing how AD is affecting your loved one is an important part of being able to support and care for them.

Decreased reasoning and judgment. Current memory is important in reasoning and judgment, so increasing memory loss makes it difficult to properly evaluate potential actions, which in turn leads to potentially harmful decisions. This inability can make it difficult to convince your loved one of the need for protective measures to keep them safe. Memory failures can also cause patients to "ignore" instructions from caregivers. While these situations can be frustrating or even scary for you as a caregiver, you must keep in mind that the person is not necessarily being stubborn, but instead has simply lost the brain tissue needed to retain the information. This means you may need to redo many things for them. For example, a person who likes to take spring water to the bathroom at bedtime may forget there is a bottle already there. Rather than scold the person, simply leave it or quietly return it. In other words, recognize the general habits of the person and do what you can to follow those as unobtrusively as possible.

This can be very frustrating, and at times you will certainly feel overwhelmed and discouraged. Remind yourself that even as you are caring for someone with AD, God cares about your situation and is caring for you (1 Peter 5:7). Use your caregiving as a way to remember all the provisions God makes for you daily without your recognizing his help. In caring for your loved one and helping to provide for their needs, you are demonstrating the character and care of Christ toward them. This is a major way that he is building his character in you, and he will provide the resources of love and renewed energy to continue caring for your loved one. Share your struggles and frustrations with your heavenly Father and ask him to renew your strength (Isaiah 40:31). Ask for his wisdom and grace and for open hearts when you must have difficult conversations with your loved one, especially if you need to impose restrictions (e.g., not allowing them to drive). He *will* be faithful to both of you. And when you are tempted to complain and grow weary (as everyone who cares for someone with AD will be at some point), ask Jesus to remind you that as you serve one of "the least of these" you are really serving Jesus (Matthew 25:40).

Decreased energy. You may also notice that your loved one has less energy and is slowing down. Increasing age automatically produces decreasing energy due to deterioration of all the processes in the body, and Alzheimer's worsens this natural progression. With decreased energy, a person's interests begin to narrow, and when loss of recent memory is added in, a person will discontinue formerly enjoyable activities and responsibilities. For example, the accountant who has kept the family finances will begin to do a bad job or show no interest in doing them. The person who has enjoyed cooking might shortcut some recipes, leading to less tasty meals. The former English teacher will begin to hesitate more before finding the correct word. This is especially true for tasks and activities that take place outside the home, as those require even more mental and physical energy. Be aware that these behaviors could be due to real physical problems, rather than simple choices. At times it may be tempting to attribute this lack of interest to laziness or irresponsibility, especially if you have become accustomed to your loved one's performing a certain task or function within the family, so be mindful that the disease may impact your loved one in unexpected ways.

Decreased conversation. As part of the brain changes in AD, your loved one's conversational spontaneity will begin to decrease, leaving limited conversation—especially about recent events. As one blog noted, "Yesterday can be difficult to recall, but yesteryear can still be totally intact."[3] Rational thinking needs the benefit of short-term memory, and when that is diminished, reasoning, judgment, and social interaction may be affected.

The Evans family noticed that Grandpa Joe often answered his visitors with shorter responses than usual. Sometimes when his responses were longer and referred to recent events they contained inaccuracies. He began to decline invitations to visit friends, excusing himself by saying he did not feel up to it. In loving concern, his son Sam gently asked if he honestly enjoyed those visits anymore. When Joe responded in the negative, Sam asked what took away the enjoyment. Joe answered that it was difficult for him to carry on a conversation because he could not remember things as they talked. Joe told his son how discouraged he was becoming by the new limitations he was experiencing and by wondering what else would change. The discussion helped Sam understand what was taking place in his father's mind.

Sam agreed that he found it difficult as well, so together they looked at a number of Scripture passages offering encouragement in difficult times. One verse they found helpful was Psalm 18:2: "The LORD is my rock and my fortress and my deliverer; My God, my strength, in whom I will trust; My shield and the horn of my salvation, my stronghold" (NKJV). It was comforting to remember that, although many things were changing for Joe, God would remain the same and would continue to offer his comfort and strength to Joe and to his family. Together Sam and Joe thanked God that this was all possible because of the freeing sacrifice of Christ on the cross. And Jesus's resurrection guaranteed that Alzheimer's would not have the final word in Joe's life. Instead he would live forever with Jesus, healed and whole. The following passages can help you and your loved one remember that your faithful Savior will sustain you through the challenges of today and tomorrow:

- "You keep him in perfect peace whose mind is stayed on you, because he trusts in you. Trust in the LORD forever, for the LORD GOD is an everlasting rock" (Isaiah 26:3–4).
- "For I consider that the sufferings of this present time are not worth comparing with the glory that is to be revealed to us" (Romans 8:18).
- "He will wipe away every tear from their eyes, and death shall be no more, neither shall there be mourning, nor crying, nor pain anymore, for the former things have passed away" (Revelation 21:4).

Decreased patience. As memory wanes and daily functions start to become more taxing, you will likely notice your loved one (and you!) struggling with impatience. Even simple tasks now take much longer to accomplish as the person has a harder time staying on task, and necessary items (keys, remote control, glasses, etc.) are often misplaced. As these things come up, remember that, while your loved one's impatient responses can make a difficult situation even more unpleasant for you, they are likely wrestling with fear in addition to their frustration at not being able to accomplish their goals. It's scary not to be able to function the way you used to, and especially not to be able to trust your own mind the way you used to.

As you struggle with your own impatience, remember that Christ offers you his endless stores of compassion and patience for your loved one. Just as Christ is patient with us in our human weakness and even when we willfully fail to follow him, you can grow in Christlike patience for your loved one's forgetfulness and even their impatience. Daily ask for the fruit of the Spirit (love, joy, peace, patience, kindness, goodness, faithfulness, gentleness, and self-control [Galatians 5:22–23]) in your life. When you see the lack of those fruits, turn to Jesus in repentance and ask for help and change. He will answer your prayer—bit by bit—as you keep going to him. As you grow in this area, you will be much more equipped to help your loved one grow in patience and faith through this trial.

Even as you deal with the spiritual side of this issue, you can look for ways to help your loved one keep better track of things. For example, work on ways to put frequently used items in places your loved one can easily find them (e.g., hanging keys on a hook by the door, putting remote controls in a basket by the television, or keeping eyeglasses on a bedside table), and help establish a routine for returning items that they can follow without thinking. It may also be helpful to establish daily routines to help with daily activities such as mealtimes and bedtimes, medication schedules, and doctor's appointments, so your loved one does not need to figure out what needs to be done and when. Having a large digital clock that also shows the date can be helpful. In order to help your loved one continue living as independently as possible,[4] you might obtain an easily used GPS for the car, even as you evaluate whether he or she should continue driving. Also take advantage of what your loved one can still do well.

And keep reminding them regularly that neither God's love nor your love for them is based on their having a sharp memory. In fact, Psalm 145:14 says, "The LORD upholds all who are falling and raises up all who are bowed down." In other words, God will be faithful to uphold them when they are weak.

Responding Well to Early- and Middle-Stage Alzheimer's

As the disease progresses, the person's abilities may fluctuate from time to time and may be affected by fatigue, medications, discomfort, etc. One day they may seem able to accomplish a given task and another day unable to do it. It helps when caregivers recognize and understand the differences between physical inability due to brain damage, and stubbornness, irresponsibility, and deliberate refusal to do certain actions.[5]

When Grandpa Joe did not want to take care of his taxes anymore, this was easy for the family to understand. He was not being lazy but was having problems with memory, making the work with numbers that had been his life just too difficult. The fact that he was late in filing taxes and an accountant was finding errors in his reports were key indicators that dealing with numbers was a problem for him. As they observed him slowing down and saw the difficulty of daily activities, they saw that his lack of interest in travel was also a natural response and not stubbornness. They began to evaluate each new change in his response through the grid of what was happening in his brain. They found encouragement in the memory of the years he has been responsible with his life and the ways God had blessed him in the process. Just as God repeatedly encouraged the Israelites to remember all he had done for them (Psalms 77:11; 105:5; 111:4; 143:5) and Peter encouraged his readers to remember God's blessings (2 Peter 1:12–13; 3:1), the family applied this to the current times when Grandpa could not do things that he once did.

Through reading the chapter "The 36-Hour Day" in the book by the same title, the family learned that multiple choices were probably overwhelming him.[6] This explained the difficulty he experienced trying to choose something from the menu at a restaurant. So they narrowed the selection down to a couple of his former favorites and ask him which he preferred. There were occasions he would choose what the person next to him chose. These situations helped the family continue to grow in Christlike patience for him. They were encouraged by remembering the many times Jesus helped the helpless and patiently guided people in their decision making (John 4:5–30; 5:6–9; Mark 10:17–22; Luke 19:1–9).

Your response to the various stages of AD should depend on the needs at that time. In the early stages, the main needs are for love, companionship, and support. As the disease progresses, your loved one will need aids to help remember important information for daily living. Remember that our call as Christians is to love one another and to be patient in trouble, so that even when your loved one is irritable and angry you can respond with acts of kindness (Romans 12:9–21). Try to remember how hard it would be for you not to be able to remember your past, people's names, and even where you put down your drink. Ask God daily to give you compassion for your loved one's struggles and also to give you the strength and patience to help.

The Later Stages

In the final stages of the disease even greater demands for help are placed on the family, and it is easy to feel overwhelmed. The time and effort needed to help your loved one slowly erodes your personal time as the caregiver. Fatigue and the required sacrifice of desired personal activities can tempt you to grumble and complain. And it's true that not only your loved one is experiencing the effects of the fall, you are as well. Perhaps you've noticed that you are feeling irritation and resentment as you struggle with the never-ending demands of caregiving. And now you feel guilty on top of everything else.

When you notice these attitudes in yourself, turn to Christ for help. He understands your life, your temptations, and your challenges intimately and offers you his grace and power. "For we do not have a high priest who is unable to sympathize with our weaknesses, but one who in every respect has been tempted as we are, yet without sin. Let us then with confidence draw near to the throne of grace, that we may receive mercy and find grace to help in time of need" (Hebrews 4:15–16). As you seek his help, begin to replace your complaints with thanksgiving. Make a list of the variety of blessings that you have received from your loved one over the years, as well as the numerous ways God is providing blessings in the present situation. Gratitude to God is a sure and sane way to overcome your negative feelings—and the more you look, the more you'll find to be grateful for. When fatigue and the pressure of providing care dominate your life, review your list and thank God for his blessings.

One of the most difficult things to deal with in the progression of Alzheimer's disease is that, as a result of memory failure, your loved one may become suspicious and make false accusations against you or other caregivers. When the keys cannot be found, the family is accused of losing them. When an appointment with the doctor is missed, the clinic is accused of changing the date and failing to inform the person of the change. These accusations can become personal. For example the person may say, "You are taking away my car because you don't love me." The family will not only be unappreciated, but may even be criticized. This can progress to open hostility toward the family, regardless of how much or how well you love the person. When you are tempted to angrily defend yourself against accusations, it is important to remember that these statements from your loved one have more to do with the brain damage they have suffered than with their actual feelings toward you. Jesus once again provides help for navigating this situation. "In your relationships with one another, have the same mindset as Christ Jesus: Who, being in very nature God, did not consider equality with God something to be used to his own advantage; rather, he made himself nothing by taking the very nature of a servant, being made in human likeness" (Philippians 2:5–7 NIV). He is the Savior who has entered into our reality and who comes alongside us in our suffering.

Christ's example of unilateral love toward us—giving one hundred percent irrespective of how much love is received—should guide your plans and actions toward your loved one. As Colossians 1:21–22 points out, "You, who once were alienated and hostile in mind, doing evil deeds, he has now reconciled in his body of flesh by his death, in order to present you holy and blameless and above reproach before him." Jesus did this because of his love for us, and this is the love you will need in order to care for your loved one with AD. Learn to see your loved one's hostile behavior as an opportunity to grow in Christlike love and sacrificial service. It will require the grace of God daily to endure rejection and even animosity from the person you love, but if you persevere in loving when it's most difficult, you will find Christ already there before you as the one who was "despised and rejected by mankind" (Isaiah 53:3 NIV).

As the Evans family watched the disease progress, it was easy to see that Grandpa Joe was becoming increasingly disabled. His increasing dependence on care from the family required more patience and flexibility from them as they took on more responsibility. Eating, personal care, communicating, and walking began to require more help from others. As they faced the strong possibility of his needing almost total round-the-clock care, they were grateful that they had studied and prepared for some of the late-stage decisions. In the earlier years, Grandpa had prepared a legal document expressing his wishes for care at the end of his life. This guided their decisions in providing an end-of-life facility for his care. They had prepared for all the legal and financial issues before he reached this stage and included in their process the search for a facility that provided the level of care that was satisfactory to them. Understanding that death usually does not occur as a direct result of the damage to the brain, but instead from failure of other organs or from infections, they wanted to make sure the facility they chose was capable of providing the medical care Joe might need. Their goal was not simply to prolong his life, but to help him be as comfortable as possible in his last days.

As they were planning, they were also praying, and Romans 15:5–6 helped in both processes. They were encouraged that "the God of endurance and encouragement grant you to live in such harmony with one another, in accord with Christ Jesus, that together you may with one voice glorify the God and Father of our Lord Jesus Christ." Holding onto this promise and praying continually, they had a number of candid discussions about the best care for Grandpa that was financially available to them. Differences were openly discussed with the understanding that Christ's love was to guide them in solutions. The gospel was a great spiritual and emotional encouragement to them during this time. As Grandpa neared the end of his life, Christ's resurrection guaranteed they would see him again, and they were able to extend Christ's love to him to the end.

Ask for and Accept Help

If you are the caregiver and/or family member of someone with AD, don't be shy about asking for and accepting help.[7] Enlisting help from family and friends is not abdicating responsibility; it is a clear recognition of personal limits. Giving care to an AD person can become extremely demanding, depending on the stage of the disease. As the AD person needs more help, the caregivers and family members need more help in providing help. Help for caregivers can include things such as caring for the home, preparing meals, doing laundry, driving to the doctor, or dealing with hostility or refusal to eat.

When you become weary in the care of your AD loved one, ask God for help as well. His Word is full of good promises to encourage and strengthen you for the long, weary journey you are on with your loved one. Your daily time of Bible reading, memorization, and prayer will help provide God's endurance and encouragement (Romans 15:5). Here are just a few of the many good promises from our Lord, who knows what it is like to be weary and burdened:

- "For it is God who works in you both to will and to do for His good pleasure" (Philippians 2:13 NKJV).
- "My flesh and my heart may fail, but God is the strength of my heart and my portion forever" (Psalm 73:26).
- God provides "the immeasurable greatness of his power toward us who believe, according to the working of his great might" (Ephesians 1:19).
- "But they who wait for the LORD shall renew their strength; they shall mount up with wings like eagles; they shall run and not be weary; they shall walk and not faint" (Isaiah 40:31).
- "The sufferings of this present time are not worth comparing with the glory that is to be revealed to us" (Romans 8:18).
- "This light momentary affliction is preparing for us an eternal weight of glory beyond all comparison, as we look not to the things that are seen but to the things that are unseen. For the things that are seen are transient, but the things that are unseen are eternal" (2 Corinthians 4:17–18).

Attending the funeral of a godly lady who had AD is one of my most encouraging memories. The pastor who officiated the funeral reminded the family that their loved one could now clearly praise God. For a considerable period of time prior to her death this had been impossible due to her AD. Now she was free from the mental and physical restrictions of AD and could praise God better than ever before. One day your loved one and you will be free of struggle and able to see God clearly and praise him for an eternity. What a hope and encouragement!

Additional Resources

General Resources on Suffering:

Piper, John and Taylor, Justin, eds. *Suffering and the Sovereignty of God.* Wheaton: Crossway, 2006.

Bridges, Jerry. *Trusting God: Even When Life Hurts.* Carol Stream, IL: Tyndale House, 2008.

Specific Resources on Alzheimer's Disease:

Mace, Nancy L. and Rabins, Peter V. *The 36-Hour Day, 5th Edition: A Family Guide to Caring for People Who Have Alzheimer Disease, Related Dementias, and Memory Loss.* Baltimore: Johns Hopkins University Press, 2011. This huge 609-page book is the most helpful and practical I've found. The title correctly describes life with an AD person. The book length only indicates its value, like having a huge treasure chest full of jewels. The chapter titled "The 36-Hour Day" is particularly helpful.

Harvard Health Publications, "A Guide to Alzheimer's Disease," http://www.health.harvard.edu/special_health_reports/a-guide-to-alzheimers-disease.

Alzheimer's Association
http://www.alz.org

Alzheimer's Foundation of America
http://www.alzfdn.org

National Institute of Health
http://www.nia.nih.gov

BrightFocus Foundation
http://www.ahaf.org

Cleveland Clinic
http://my.clevelandclinic.org/disorders/Alzheimers_
Disease/hic_Alzheimers_and_Dementia_Overview.
aspx

Mayo Clinic
http://www.mayoclinic.com/health/
alzheimers-disease/DS00161/tab=InDepth

Caregiver guide from National Institute of Health
http://www.nia.nih.gov/alzheimers/publication/
caregiver-guide

Endnotes

1. Alzheimer's Association, "What Is Alzheimer's?", http://www.alz.org/alzheimers_disease_what_is_alzheimers .asp.

2. Alzheimer's Association, "Early-Stage Caregiving," http://www.alz.org/care/alzheimers-early-mild-stage-caregiving.asp.

3. Alzheimer's Association, "Preserving Memories," http://www.alzheimersblog.org/2013/10/24/preserving-memories/.

4. Alzheimer's Association, "Early-Stage Caregiving," http://www.alz.org/care/alzheimers-early-mild-stage-caregiving.asp.

5. N. L. Mace, R. V. Rabins, *The 36-Hour Day* (Johns Hopkins University Press, 2011), chapter "The 36-Hour Day," 35–77.

6. Ibid.

7. Michael A. Emlet, *Help for the Caregiver* (Greensboro: New Growth Press, 2005). This minibook contains many helpful resources for handling the difficulties of long-term caregiving.

Simple, Quick, Biblical

Advice on Complicated Counseling Issues
for Pastors, Counselors, and Individuals

MINIBOOK
CATEGORIES

- Personal Change
- Marriage & Parenting
- Medical & Psychiatric Issues
- Women's Issues
- Singles
- Military

USE YOURSELF | GIVE TO A FRIEND | DISPLAY IN YOUR CHURCH OR MINISTRY

New Growth Press

Go to **www.newgrowthpress.com** or call **336.378.7775** to purchase individual minibooks or the entire collection. Durable acrylic display stands are also available to house the minibook collection.